40400

Gorseinon Col

Learning Resou ce Centre

Belgrave Road : Gorseinon : Swansea : SA4 ᴜʀᴅ Tel: (01792) 890731

This ⌐ s **YOUR RESPONSIBILITY** and is due for
renewal on or before the last date shown.

.914 STE **ACC. NO.** 40400

⌐45

Methuen Drama

Published by Methuen 2003

First published in 2003 by
Methuen Publishing Ltd
215 Vauxhall Bridge Road
London SW1V 1EJ

·

www.methuen.co.uk

Copyright © Simon Stephens 2003

The author has asserted his moral rights

Methuen Publishing Ltd reg. number 3543167

ISBN 0 413 77365 5

A CIP catalogue record for this book is available at the British Library

Typeset by SX Composing DTP, Rayleigh, Essex
Transferred to digital printing 2004

Caution
All rights whatsoever in this play are strictly reserved.
Enquiries about rights for amateur and professional performances should be
directed to: Casarotto Ramsay and Associates Ltd, 60-66 Wardour Street,
London W1V 4ND. No performance may be given unless a licence has been
obtained.

This paperback is sold subject to the condition that it shall not, by way of
trade or otherwise, be lent, resold, hired out or otherwise circulated without the
publisher's prior consent in any form of binding or cover other than that in which
it is published and without a similar condition including this condition being
imposed on the subsequent purchaser.

the production

atc and sheffield theatres present

One Minute

by Simon Stephens

Season Sponsor

cast and production team

di gary burroughs	simon wolfe
dc robert evans	tom ellis
dr anne schults	teresa banham
marie louise burdett	lucy black
catherine denham	sarah paul

director	gordon anderson
designer	anthony macilwaine
composer	julian swales
lighting designer	nigel edwards

production manager	rob mckinney
company stage manager	gareth baston
technical stage manager	kieran dicker
studio co-ordinator	cath booth
(sheffield theatres)	

graphic design	david whiteley

executive producer	emma dunton
administrators	lydia nelson/jenni kershaw

properties, scenery and costumes are made in the
sheffield theatres workshops

with special thanks to hetty shand and rebecca manson-jones

first performed at the crucible studio, sheffield 6 june 2003

**the play is written for ben, sara and archie.
it is also dedicated to laura**

biographies

GORDON ANDERSON
director

Gordon is Artistic Director of ATC.
He has directed productions for some of the UK's leading theatre and opera
companies including English Touring Opera, the Royal Court theatre, Scottish
Opera, Manchester Royal Exchange, the Lyric Theatre Hammersmith, Broomhill
Opera and the Bristol Old Vic. He has also worked on development projects for
Channel 4, BBC, Alamo, Carlton and Tiger Aspect.

TERESA BANHAM
dr anne schults

Teresa's theatre and television credits include The Shawl (Sheffield Crucible), My
Best Friend (Hampstead), Snake in the Grass (Old Vic), The Herbal Bed, The White
Devil (RSC), Here (Donmar Warehouse). Television includes Redcaps, The Project,
Touch and Go, Out of Hours, Roughnecks, The Healer (BBC), Trust (Box TV),
Monsignor Renard, The Bill (Carlton), The Six Sides of Steve Coogan (Pozzitive
Prods) Teresa received the Best Actress award in the London Fringe and M.E.N
Awards for her portrayal of Anna in Shared Experience's Anna Karenina.

GARETH BASTON
company stage manager

Since graduating from Rose Bruford College with a degree in Stage Management
Gareth has worked in Rep at the Belgrade, Coventry and at the Dukes, Lancaster
on their Outdoor Promenade Seasons. On tour he has worked with Out of Joint
(international tour), Kneehigh, Oxford Stage, Pop- Up, Theatre Centre and Method
and Madness. In London he has worked at the Donmar, The Arts Theatre and at
the top of Euston Tower for Deborah Warner. He also works regularly for Raymond
Gubbay at the Albert Hall, Birmingham Indoor Arena and on tour.

LUCY BLACK
mane louise burdett

Lucy trained at the Bristol Old Vic Theatre School. Recent theatre includes the New
Writer's Festival (Gate Theatre), Stigmata (National Studio), Twelfth Night, Measure
for Measure, King Lear, Coriolanus, Midsummer Nights Dream (Tobacco Factory), A
Tender Prayer, Seed of the Bauhinia (Bristol Old Vic), Blue Remembered Hills
(Pleasance, Edinburgh), Tomorrow is a Lovely Day (B.A.C). Television includes
Holby, Doctors, Murder in Mind, Casualty (BBC), The Hereafter (ITV), Moll Flanders
(Granada).

biographies

KIERAN DICKER
technical stage manager

Kieren started working in theatre ten years ago with the intention of saving a little extra money to travel the world with. Those who work in the arts won't be surprised to find out he's still saving. For the past 2 1/2 years he has been touring with The Reduced Shakespeare Company extensively throughout the U.K. and recently in Holland. Before this he worked and trained at the Old Town Hall Theatres in Hemel Hempstead.

EMMA DUNTON
executive producer

Before joining ATC Emma worked at Volcano Theatre Company producing shows and managing the national and international tour of Macbeth-Director's Cut, The Town That Went Mad, and Private Lives in Russia, Sri Lanka, Spain, Austria, Lithuania, Albania, Slovakia and Kosovo amongst others. Since joining ATC in July 2001 Emma has produced In The Solitude Of Cotton Fields, Arabian Night, Out Of Our Heads and the Theatrelab education project. Previously she has worked at the British Council and on low-budget feature films in Los Angeles.

NIGEL EDWARDS
lighting designer

For the last 13 years Nigel has been designing for Forced Entertainment from Some Confusions... to The Voices. Premieres include Debbie Green's Dirty Butterfly; (Soho Theatre),Sarah Kane's Cleansed and 4.48 Psychosis for the Royal Court Theatre, Crave, Riddance, Sleeping Around, The Cosmonauts Last Message... and Splendour also for Paines Plough and Arabian Night and The Boy Who Left Home for ATC. Other work includes Sexual Perversity in Chicago; (Comedy Theatre), Roberto Zucco, The Tempest and Victoria for RSC, Inconceivable for West Yorkshire Playhouse, Clare de Luz for Insomniac, Pigg in Hell and Total Massala Slammer for Remote Control.

TOM ELLIS
dc robert evans

Tom is from Sheffield and trained at the RSAMD in Glasgow. His extensive screen work includes the regular role of Ricky Tomlinson's would-be son Frank in the BBC's Nice Guy Eddie. Other tv roles include John Browdie in Nicholas Nickleby (ITV), Tim in Pollyanna (ITV) and the guest lead of Marko in Linda Green (BBC). His most recent film credit is for the forthcoming Family Business directed by Craig Ferguson. He will start work on a role in the new Mike Leigh film this summer. Tom was last on stage in a production of Shangalang for the Chichester Festival Theatre

biographies

JENNI KERSHAW
administrator

Jenni joined ATC as an intern in March 2003 and took over as administrator in May. She completed a BA in English Literature and Theology at Liverpool University (Chester College) whilst gaining work experience at The Gateway Theatre in Chester. She is currently studying for an MA in Arts Administration and Cultural Policy at Goldsmiths.

ANTHONY MACILWAINE
designer

Anthony has designed productions for a range of well-known companies. His most recent designs were Iron and Quartz for the Traverse. Other designs include: The Mikado (Grange Park Opera); Making Noise Quietly (Oxford Stage Company); Wozzeck, From the House of Dead (Long Beach Opera); Beauty and the Beast (Young Vic); Prayers of Sherkin (Old Vic); Euripides Trilogy; Aurelie My Sister; Danton's Death, Agamemmon's Children, The Lovers, The Cheating Hearts (The Gate); Peribanez (Arts Theatre, Cambridge); Loot (Magnificent Theatre Co); Dark Ride (Soho Rep, New York); Grimm Tales (Leicester Haymarket); Await the Tide (Edinburgh Festival).

LYDIA NELSON
administrator

Lydia joined ATC in September 2002, having just completed an MA in Arts Administration and Cultural Policy at Goldsmiths. During her time at Goldsmiths Lydia worked on the Musical Futures festival at Greenwich Theatre. Prior to this she was involved in various aspects of student theatre in Cambridge.

SARAH PAUL
catherine denham

Sarah trained at Central School of Speech and Drama. Sarah recently completed shooting Silent Witness and Eastenders. Other television work includes Doctors, Casualty, Judge John Deed (BBC). Theatre credits include Who's Harry (Pleasance), Arcadia, Marisol, Rape Upon Rape, Trumpets and Drums, Twelfth Night, The Cherry Orchard (Central). Sarah won the 2001 Carlton Hobbs Bursary and a six-month contract with BBC Radio Drama.

biographies

SIMON STEPHENS
writer

Simon's plays for theatre include Bluebird (Royal Court Theatre, London 1998 directed by Gordon Anderson); Herons (Royal Court Theatre, London 2001; Staats theatre Stuttgart 2003); Port (Royal Exchange Theatre, Manchester 2002). His radio plays include Five Letters Home To Elizabeth (BBC Radio 4, 2001) and Digging (BBC Radio 4 2003). Awards include Arts Council Resident Dramatist at the Royal Court Theatre, 2000. Pearson Award for Best Play 2001 for Port; nomination for Olivier Award for most promising playwright for Herons 2001. His film Jackdaw is currently under commission from BBC Films. He is also under commission from the Royal Court theatre and the Royal Exchange Theatre. He is the Writers Tutor at the Young Writers Programme of the Royal Court theatre.

JULIAN SWALES
composer

Julian Swales was the guitarist in 90s alt- rock band Kitchens of Distinction. On four albums for One Little Indian Records they produced music that encompassed both heartfelt songwriting and sonic noise experimentalism. Though critically acclaimed in the UK, commercial success was mostly found in the USA and they toured there extensively. Julian gave up performing in the late 90s to concentrate solely on studio-based composition and now he writes mainly for film, television, theatre and contemporary dance. His most recent score was Everest for the BBC. A Kitchens Of Distinction retrospective, Capsule, was released in April.

SIMON WOLFE
di gary burroughs

Simon trained at Central School of Speech and Drama. His most recent theatre includes Great Expectations (Bristol Old Vic); As The Beast Sleeps (Tricycle Theatre); The Weir (Number One Tour); The Force Of Change (The Royal Court); Wonderful Tennessee (Lyric Theatre Belfast); Outside On The Street (Gate Theatre); Waiting For Godot (Teatro Nationale, Milan). Simon's television credits include The Great Kandinsky (BBC Screen One) and The Bill (ITV).

writer's notes

Ever since I started writing for theatre I have been in awe of good actors. Both in rehearsal and in performance I love watching them work. There is little, in my professional life, as exciting or as flattering as watching words that I have written being given a life and an energy in the rehearsal room or on stage. Some of the time I write for actors. When I write a scene I don't see discrete, self contained, fictional characters in my head, I see actors, specific actors, becoming those characters. So Gordon Anderson's idea, at the start of 2001 that I should write a play for the Actors Touring Company, a play that would be developed and devised with him and with a group of actors in rehearsal seemed to make a huge amount of sense to me. The work that we did over the course of the next twelve months I found rewarding and exciting, I would go into the workshops each morning with a tangible feeling of anticipation at the work to come. I hope I have done that work justice in my play.

We both knew two things, Gordon and I, before we even contacted any actors. Firstly we wanted to write about London. Its chaos and its coherence, its coincidences and its elusiveness, its brutality and its generosity. We also thought that London, as a subject, demanded a new narrative structure. So we knew that we wanted to experiment with the traditional Anglo-American theatrical narrative form in which I was certainly deeply steeped. We wanted to take our lead from some of the contemporary European playwrights, Roland Schimmelpfennig, Bernard Marie Koltes, Franz Xavier Kroetz, Jon Fosse, David Guisellman those playwrights that both of us had been reading and Gordon was excited about producing with ATC to find a new form of telling the stories that we developed. A form that had an immediacy and a formal boldness more reflective of life in London at the start of a new millennium.

We took those two things into all of our workshops. Over the course of the next twelve months we met three times with three different groups of actors. In August and December of 2001 we worked with actors from the Actors Centre to perfect our process. Taking acting techniques and improvisational games that Gordon had nurtured and writing exercises that I had learned and developed at the Young Writers Programme of the Royal Court theatre we experimented with new ways of triggering scenes. We worked with memories and with music, with random ways of selecting locations from our collective knowledge of the city, with objects and with pictures as starting points for improvisations. We went out for walks to places we had never been to before. We got actors to improvise scenes in absolute silence in which they only gradually came to understand the world which we had placed them into. We developed tableaux, wrote monologues, conducted interviews, eavesdropped. We amassed a load of material during each of these weeks. At the end of each of them we had developed small sequences of scenes which we felt were leading us in the right direction.

writer's notes cont'd

And at the start of this year we took these processes back to the studio of the Actors Touring Company and employed a company of actors to run through them with us one more time. The material from this final week-long workshop proved to be the main source of inspiration for 'One Minute'.

There were other things.

I am an inveterate walker and this play gave me an excuse to walk for miles and miles. I circumnavigated the circle line and more on two or three occasions. I spent one day travelling tube trains from nine thirty until nine thirty and looking at those areas I had only ever seen on Underground maps before. I took photographs, and made detailed notes everywhere I went.

I read plays: Caryl Churchill's 'This Is A Chair'; David Grieg's 'A Cosmonaut Sends His Final Message Home To the Woman He Once Loved In The Former Soviet Union'; Martin Crimp's 'Attempts On her Life'; Peter Gill's 'Cardiff East'. I also read writing about London - Iain Sinclair's 'Lights Out For The Territory'; Peter Ackroyd's 'London - A Biography'; Christopher Ross's 'Tunnel Visions' were particularly important in my attempt to make sense of the material we were amassing.

I listened to music. One actress played me Gavin Bryars' 'Jesus Blood Never Failed Me Yet' for the first time in ten years and I ended up listening to that and (for other reasons) Bonnie Prince Billy's heart-stopping 'At the Break Of Day' every morning before I wrote.

I watched films - Atom Egoyan's 'Exotica'; Kieslowski's 'Three Colours:Blue' and John Sayles' 'Lone Star' were all invaluable. The last three chosen in part because their subject matter - how we grieve and how we console the grieving was clearly becoming the subject of my play.

In my own life and in the world I saw around me, 2001 felt like a year of grief. London, with its sense of isolation and latent connectedness, felt like an appropriate context against which to analyse questions of how we console the inconsolable. It is a coincidence typical to this city and fitting to our initial objectives that the improvisations that the actors developed in January of this year, even when they were unplanned and instinctive, should circle around the same questions I had been asking myself for the past six months, the same ideas I wanted to write about. Those questions, I hope, are synthesised, in my play.

atc

ATC, now in its 23rd year, is committed to touring the most exciting and innovative contemporary work from the UK and international repertoire to all areas of the country. Since Gordon Anderson took over as Artistic Director in 2001, ATC has created new working relationships throughout the world and embarked on an eclectic programme involving collaborations with some of the most vibrant of the UK's emerging theatre and comedy writers, designers and choreographers. ATC's most recent production was a narrative comedy-drama, OUT OF OUR HEADS with comedy duo SUSAN AND JANICE.

We have a number of exciting projects in the pipeline. This autumn we are co-producing the black comedy, EXCUSES! by Joel Joan and Jordi Sanchez with the Barcelona based production company KRAMPACK. In the spring of 2004 we will be producing JEFF KOONS by contemporary German playwright Rainald Goetz.

'...the brilliant London-based company ATC.. suddenly floods that same space with a great lost world of rich colour, intense flavour, howling passion, sudden violence and sweet erotic magic.'

The Scotsman on Arabian Night

alford house, aveline st, london, SE11 5DQ
t: 020 7735 8311   f: 020 7735 1031
e: atc@atc-online.com   www.atc-online.com

Registered charity number 279 458   ATC is funded by Arts Council England

sheffield theatres - awards

The Peter Gill festival, Crucible Studio
Peter Brook Empty Space Award Winner 2002

Best Musical, High Society
Barclays TMA Regional Theatre Awards
(nomination)

Theatre of the Year 2001
Barclays TMA Regional Theatre Awards

Best Actress, Victoria Hamilton, As You Like It
Barclays TMA Regional Theatre Awards

Best Director, Michael Grandage, As You Like It
Evening Standard Theatre Awards

Best Director, Michael Grandage, As You Like It
The Critic's Circle Award

As You Like It
The South Bank Show Award for Theatre

Financial Times/Arts & Business Awards
(shortlisted)

Victoria Hamilton in
As You Like It
2000

Photograph. Simon Warner

Joseph Fiennes in
Edward II
2001

Photograph· Ivan Kyncl

Matt Bardock and
Justin Salinger in
Kick for Touch
2002

Photograph Simon Annand

about sheffield theatres

Sheffield Theatres is the largest theatre complex outside London, offering a wide range of performances from drama to dance, comedy to musicals.

The Crucible Theatre, built in 1971 houses a thrust stage and is the main producing venue in the complex. Recently awarded the Barclays Theatre of the Year Award, productions have included a new version of Iphigenia by Edna O'Brien and Amanda Donohoe in Teeth 'n' Smiles, both directed by Anna Mackmin, Philip Pullman's work on stage for the first time in Stephen Russell's adaptation of The Firework-Maker's Daughter directed by Paul Hunter and Hayley Carmichael, Sweet Charity directed by Timothy Sheader, and Derek Jacobi in The Tempest, Kenneth Branagh in Richard III, Tom Hollander in Don Juan, Joseph Fiennes in Edward II and Victoria Hamilton in As You Like It, all directed by Sheffield Theatres' Associate Director Michael Grandage.

The Lyceum Theatre, built in 1897, receives the country's top touring productions including visits by the National Theatre, The Royal Shakespeare Company, Opera North, Northern Ballet Theatre and hit shows from the West End.

The Studio Theatre is a flexible 'black box' space playing host to smaller touring companies, contemporary dance and the world famous Lindsays and Friends Chamber Music Festivals. Recently awarded the Peter Brook Empty Space Award, Sheffield Theatres productions in the Studio have included Could It Be Magic? (with Unlimited Theatre), Macbeth adapted and directed by James Phillips and the Peter Gill Festival.

Kenneth Branagh in
Richard III
2002

Derek Jacobi in
The Tempest
2002

Amanda Donohoe in
Teeth n Smiles
2002

Photographs: Ivan Kyncl

the square circle

Sheffield Theatres operates a flexible membership scheme that not only rewards frequent theatre goers but also encourages young first-time attenders. Benefits include:

- A range of membership levels to suit every need and budget
- Generous ticket discounts
- Priority booking
- Talks, tours and opportunities to meet the acting companies and production teams
- Regular newsletter and brochure mailings
- Members' Hotline

For further information contact Alison Moore:
Tel: 0114 249 6007/email: a.moore@sheffieldtheatres.co.uk

education

Sheffield Theatres Education Programme actively engages people in the work of the theatre through a varied and challenging programme of activities and events. It is designed for all those who wish to understand and discover more about the process of creating theatre. The Education Programme reflects the rich cultural diversity of its community and encourages access and inclusion. It includes:

- Theatre in schools and community venues
- Youth theatre and projects with young people
- Special education projects with the early years, schools and colleges, and the community
- Education Programmes supporting Sheffield Theatres productions including talks, a range of workshops, and resource packs
- Backstage tours and specialist tours
- Work experience and student placements
- Training and development programmes for teachers and education workers

For further information contact Sue Burley, Education Administrator on 0114 249 5999 or visit www.sheffieldtheatres.co.uk/education.

One Minute

For Ben, Sara and Archie.
And dedicated also to Laura.

Characters

DI Gary Burroughs, *thirty-eight*
DC Robert Evans, *twenty-four*
Dr Anne Schults, *thirty-six*
Marie Louise Burdett, *twenty-seven*
Catherine Denham, *twenty-one*

One Minute was written after a series of workshops with
actors from the Actors Centre, London, and the Actors
Touring Company, London, led by Gordon Anderson.
Without their help this play could not have been written.

I am also indebted to DI Graham Macfarlane and PC
Peter de Winton for their help in researching the piece.

Setting

The play is set in a variety of locations in London, over the course of 2001.

The set should be as spare as possible.

A character who plays in two consecutive scenes need not wait to arrive in any second setting before playing the second scene. Rather the scenes can bleed, quite quickly, into one another.

The characters should remain on stage throughout.

The dates could be displayed or announced before each section starts.

During the blackouts the silhouettes of the characters should become gradually clear.

The silences could be punctuated. Perhaps brief, intrusive, warning beeps. The kind of sound that fax machines make when they run out of paper.

A dash (–) after a word denotes an interruption or an inability to speak or complete a word or sentence. An ellipsis (. . .) denotes a trailing off.

January

Blackout. Ten seconds.

A clothes shop on High Street Kensington. Midday. **Marie Louise Burdett** *and* **Catherine Denham**. **Marie Louise** *stares at an unnoticing* **Catherine** *for some time before she speaks to her. She is holding a T-shirt. Holds it away from herself. Looks at it through light.*

Marie Louise   What do you think?

Catherine   I think it suits you.

Marie Louise (*looking away*)   I'm not sure.

Catherine   It's very simple. In a good way. Not, y'know, not flashy.

Marie Louise   No.

Catherine   I think it's really smart.

Long pause. **Catherine** *turns from her.*

Marie Louise   I hate this. All . . . this.

Catherine   Yeah.

Marie Louise   Do you know what I mean?

Catherine   Yes.

Very long pause. **Catherine** *turns to watch her.*

Marie Louise (*about another T-shirt*)   But this I like.

Catherine   Oh yes.

Marie Louise   This is very good.

Marie Louise *smells the T-shirt.*

Catherine   It works.

Marie Louise   I'm sorry?

Catherine   I said it works. I don't think you should look further. It works.

Marie Louise   How much is it?

Catherine   I've no idea.

Marie Louise   Can't you look it up?

Catherine   I'm sorry?

Marie Louise   Can't you look it up? Don't you have a, a, a, a, a book or something? A book you could look the price up in?

Catherine   I don't work here.

Marie Louise   I'm sorry?

Catherine   I said I don't work here. I'm just, I'm looking for clothes too. I don't actually, this isn't my job.

Marie Louise   Oh my God. I'm so sorry. That's God, that's, that's, that's, that's –

Catherine   It's all right.

Marie Louise   No. That's terrible. How embarrassing. I honestly didn't think. I mean I thought. I wasn't thinking. Clearly. I mean clearly. Well. Where is everybody?

Catherine   I don't know.

Marie Louise   There's nobody here.

Catherine   I know.

Marie Louise   I could just walk out with this.

Catherine   Are you crying?

Marie Louise   What?

Catherine   Don't cry. It's all right.

Marie Louise   I'm not crying! For God's sake!

She examines the garment.

I don't even think there's, is there a little, one of those, is there a tag or anything? A magnetic strip or anything? I don't think there is. I could just walk out of the door and take this and nobody would know. There aren't any even any cameras even. These shops. I mean. These shops. Sometimes, do you ever get the feeling? You come in here. Come into one of these places and you want to be sick.

Catherine   I'm not sure.

Marie Louise (*turning to* **Catherine**)   I wanted something to wear so that if I went out I could run. Just go out and run. And now there isn't even a girl here.

Catherine   Maybe you should take it.

Marie Louise   To take my money or or or or or anything.

Catherine   Maybe you should.

Marie Louise   What?

Catherine   Just take it.

Marie Louise   I couldn't. It would just –

She stops and stares at **Catherine**.

Catherine (*staring back at her, seriously*)   I think you should.

Dr Anne Schults's *garden in west Camden. Afternoon.* **DI Gary Burroughs** *and* **Dr Anne Schults**. *Drinking cups of coffee. She looks at him intently.*

Anne   Do you miss her?

Gary   I'd like to see her more often, yeah.

Anne   Why don't you?

Gary   It's not always easy.

Anne   Do you see your parents ever?

Gary   I see my mum from time to time. My dad died when I was a kid.

Anne   How old?

Gary (*turning to her*)   How . . .?

Anne   How old were you when your dad died?

Gary   Thirteen.

Anne   I'm sorry.

Gary   That's all right. It was, yer know, yer kind of don't get it, do you? (*He finishes his coffee.*) I should –

Anne   Do you ever get back home?

Gary   Not, no. No.

He tries to put the coffee cup down. Can't find anywhere to put it.

Anne   Funny, isn't it?

Gary   What?

Anne   The way people grow.

Gary (*moving to stand*)   I –

Anne   What do you think about?

Gary   I'm sorry?

Anne   When you close your eyes and you think about your home, what do you think about?

He looks at her before he answers and then sits.

Gary   Listen, Dr Schults –

Anne   Anne.

Gary   Yes –

Anne   Where did you go on holiday?

Gary   Where –

Anne   When you were a child, where did you go?

Gary (*smiling at her*)   We used to go to Peel. On the Isle of Man.

Anne   Did you enjoy it?

Gary   I loved it. Yeah.

Anne   Do you ever go back?

Gary   Not for years.

Anne   You should.

Pause. He looks up. She watches him. He taps his coffee cup in the palm of his hand.

Gary   I sometimes think it would be good to move there. Take Jenny.

Very long pause. She smiles at him. Looks away smiling.

I should be going.

Anne   Do you think I should go back to work?

Gary   It's up to you.

Anne   Is there a, a, a common, a common protocol about when it's wise for people to go back to work in circumstances like this?

Gary   Not really. No.

Anne   It gives me a tremendous sense of power and of importance and of worth.

Gary   That sounds –

Anne   It's been four days, Gary.

Gary   Yes.

Anne *looks away from him.*

Anne   I think you're very professional.

Gary   Thank you.

Anne   You seem quite compassionate.

Gary   I don't –

Anne (*looking back at him*)   Don't go.

Silence.

My husband can barely speak. I want him to.

Pause.

Every day she changes. Grows.

Pause.

The idea that she is in pain. Or, or, or, or crying even.

Pause.

A car parked outside a house in Hackney. Afternoon. **Gary Burroughs** *and* **Robert Evans** *watch the house.* **Gary** *is eating a burger wrapped in paper. He has a mouth full of food. Some time.*

Robert   How long do you think we'll be here?

Gary   Yer can never tell.

Long pause. **Robert** *looks over to* **Gary**. *He thinks about lighting a cigarette. Is interrupted.*

You got family up there still?

Robert   Mum and Dad are up there. Still where I was born. Same house. My brother moved just down the road.

Gary   How old's he?

Robert   Twenty-two. Two years younger than me.

Gary (*half looks at him*)   You twenty-four?

Robert   Yeah.

Gary   Really?

Robert   Yeah.

Gary   Yer don't look twenty-four.

Robert   Don't I?

Gary   No.

Robert   How old do I look?

Gary (*very definite*)   Twenty-one.

Pause.

Robert   Fuck off.

Gary   How do you get on with him, your brother?

Robert (*tapping his unlit cigarette on its packet*)   He's all right.
He's a bit of a mummy's boy. Always, he was always the
centre of attention with everything.

Gary   I see.

Robert (*turning to* **Gary**)   Is it always like this?

Gary (*staring at the house*)   Not always.

Robert   How long has it been now?

Gary (*not checking*)   Two hours. Keep watching.

Robert (*looking back*)   He wouldn't really have gone, would
he?

Gary   It would be unusual. But not, completely, you
know, impossible.

Gary *yawns in the car seat. He stretches, cramping* **Robert**.

Robert   Makes me sick.

Gary   What?

Robert   Thinking about it.

Gary   Yeah. That doesn't go.

Beat.

Robert   Does she not want Family Liaison?

Gary   No.

Robert   How come?

Gary   What do you mean? Not everybody does, Robert.

Robert   Why not?

Gary   Why do yer think?

Robert   It just means we end up doing the liaison, doing surveillance, doing paperwork, doing everything.

Gary (*looking at him first; some time*)   I'm not even gonna answer that.

Some more time.

Robert   I love it down here. Better than up there.

Gary   Got a good place?

Robert   Yeah. Nice. Small but, you know.

Gary (*finishing his burger*)   Whereabouts?

Robert   Up East Finchley.

Gary   You living on your own?

Robert   No. No. My girlfriend came down with me.

Gary   Oh yeah?

Robert   Esther.

Gary   What's she like?

Robert   She's . . . You know? She's very blonde. She's, I sometimes think she's quite naive. And she keeps telling me stuff. To do stuff. And getting worried about the prices of things, but she's all right.

Gary (*licking ketchup off his thumbs*)   She the one, you think?

Robert   The what?

Gary   The one. The big one. For you.

Robert Fuck off.

Gary No?

Robert (*looking to* **Gary**)   I don't know. You never know, do you.

Gary You never do.

Robert You married?

Gary I am. Keep watching.

Silence. **Robert** *lights his cigarette.* **Gary** *looks for somewhere to put his burger paper. Finds nowhere. Puts it on the back seat.* **Gary** *looks at* **Robert**.

You want another coffee?

Robert Yeah. Thank you.

Gary There's something I wanted to tell you.

Robert Oh yeah?

Gary Wait here.

Gary *leaves* **Robert** *alone. Seventeen seconds. Comes back with two cups of coffee.*

Robert This is a shit street, isn't it?

Gary What?

Robert Shit houses. Shit shops. Shit cars. Shit fucking people.

Gary Robert.

Robert Yeah.

Gary I wanted to tell you.

Robert What?

Gary You're doing all right.

Robert What?

Gary   You. You can calm down. You're doing fine.

Robert   You what?

Gary   You don't need to worry so much.

Robert   I wasn't worrying.

Gary   Good. (*He smiles at him.*) I was twenty.

Robert   Twenty.

Gary   Yeah.

Some time. **Robert** *looks at him.*

Robert   You still enjoy it?

Gary   Enjoy it?

Robert   This.

Gary   I don't know.

Robert   You love it, I bet.

Gary   I wish I didn't have to do it.

Gary *looks at him and so* **Robert** *returns to watching the house.* **Gary** *watches too.*

Robert   You never. You'd go crazy.

Gary   Live by the seaside.

Robert   Yeah?

Gary   Go to live on the Isle of Man.

Robert   Yeah?

Gary   I'd love that.

Pause. **Robert** *springs up. Puts out his cigarette.*

Robert   Is that him?

Gary   What?

Robert   There!

Gary   Where?

Robert   Up there!

Gary   Yeah. That's him.

Robert   Let's go.

Gary (*holding his arm back*)   Just. Wait.

Marie Louise Burdett's *flat. Evening.* **Marie Louise** *and* **Robert**. *He has arrived to interview her.*

Marie Louise   Are you?

Robert   Miss Burdett? I'm Detective Constable Robert Evans. Can I come in?

Marie Louise   I've been waiting all morning.

Robert   I gather you have some information regarding the search for Daisy Schults.

Marie Louise   They rang me first thing. Told me you'd be coming round.

Robert   Thank you for getting in touch.

Marie Louise   I wasn't sure that it was relevant.

Robert   Every call, Miss Burdett, I'm sure you understand, is highly appreciated.

Marie Louise   Yes. Yes. Yes. Yes. Can I get you something to drink or . . .?

Robert   I'm fine. No. Thank you. Miss Burdett, there is a series of questions I need to ask you before I can take your statement.

Marie Louise   Yes. Of course.

He pulls a notebook out of his pocket. Is just about to start writing.

I've been so scared.

Robert   I'm sorry?

Marie Louise   No. I'm sorry. I'm being . . . (*Pause.*) I'm making myself some tea, some iced tea. Are you sure you wouldn't like some?

Robert   Maybe just a coffee. If that's not inconvenient.

Marie Louise   Fine, no, no, no, of course.

She makes coffee and tea. He pulls a pen out of his pocket. He waits, watches her. He checks out her flat. Clocks the furniture. Maybe touches things. She talks as she prepares their drinks. He doesn't look at her while she talks.

I've been watching the television all week. It's terrible.

Robert   Yes. It is.

Marie Louise   Makes you think.

Gives him his drink. Takes hers. Sits. He remains standing.

I've been here, been living here, on my own, in this flat, for what, for three months. It's too big is one thing. The flat is too big. It just, well, it is, it is, it . . .

Robert   It's very smart.

Marie Louise   Thank you.

They smile at each other.

I'm going to hire out one of the rooms. I think. Find somebody. I think I know who I'm going to ask. I don't want to advertise.

Robert   No.

Marie Louise   I hear noises. In the night-time. Sometimes it sounds like it's people inside my room. It can't be, can it?

Robert   I don't –

Marie Louise I saw her photograph. They showed it on the news. At the weekend, I was watching the news. And they showed her photograph.

Robert Yes.

Marie Louise It's been five days now, hasn't it?

Robert Four.

Marie Louise I'm sorry. I'm actually finding this quite difficult.

Robert That's fine. That's very common.

Marie Louise How old is she?

Robert She's eleven years old.

Marie Louise She looks younger than that.

Robert Yes.

Marie Louise I saw her. Two nights ago.

He stares at her. Puts down his coffee cup. She won't shake his gaze.

Panatica's café, Camden. Night. **Catherine** *is clearing up.* **Gary** *is chatting to her while she works. Drinking a bottle of beer. While she talks,* **Catherine** *works, wiping tables, collecting cups, saucers, bottles, plates, glasses, waste. Returning them to her counter.* **Gary** *watches her throughout.*

Catherine We used to talk about everything.

Gary Yeah?

Catherine You could, we could just tell each other. Tell what each other was thinking half the time.

Gary That's good.

Catherine It was. Yeah. It was good. (*Beat.*) What about you?

Gary Can I get another drink?

She looks at him. They grin at each other.

Go on.

Catherine (*smiling, going back to work*)   Till's off.

Gary   Just leave it in the drawer.

Catherine   I can't. He'd kill us.

Gary   Who?

Catherine   Fat twat.

Gary   He wouldn't.

Catherine   You don't know him.

Gary   He's not so bad.

Catherine   You have no idea.

Pause. **Gary** *drains his bottle.*

How was work?

Gary *smiles at her.*

Gary   It passed.

Catherine   You always say that.

Gary   Say what?

Catherine   Never tell us anything. I always ask you how work was and you never tell us anything about it.

Gary   It's not that interesting.

Catherine   I think it is.

Gary   Most of the day today I spent sitting in a car in Hackney.

Catherine   Why?

Gary   Waiting for this guy to come back home.

Catherine   And did he?

Gary Eventually.

Catherine What had he done?

Gary (*goes to drink and realises his bottle is empty*) You don't want to know.

Catherine Yeah I do. Tell us.

Gary (*swings round on his chair to look back at her*) How was college?

Catherine Spoilsport.

Gary How was college?

Catherine It was good.

Gary What were you doing?

Catherine Lectures.

Gary What about?

Catherine Shakespeare.

Gary I used to love Shakespeare. Get us a beer.

The tables cleared, **Catherine** *moves back behind her counter and starts cashing the till. Putting coins and notes into separate bags. Counting the money.*

Catherine No.

Gary I was shit at school.

Catherine Were you?

Gary Spent all my time fighting and having sex.

Catherine Fuck off.

Gary It's true. Nearly got expelled when I was fifteen.

Catherine I don't believe you.

Gary How's the flat-hunting?

Catherine Shocking.

Gary   Yeah?

Catherine   Killing me, I'm telling yer.

Gary   Don't let it.

Catherine (*stops work, looks up*)   Can I ask you something?

Gary   Go on.

Catherine   Do you like your job?

Gary   Sometimes.

Catherine   What do you like about it?

Gary   I quite like the car chases.

Catherine   Do you?

Gary   Watching people jumping to the side of the road. That's quite funny.

Catherine   Monkey.

Gary   I used to quite like a lot of the scrotes.

Catherine   Really?

Gary   When I was a bobby. A lot of them were quite funny. Got a good, you know, good sense of humour. Now there's not so much to like.

Catherine   No?

Gary   No. Different class of criminal. A lot . . .

Catherine   What?

Gary   I'm not gonna persuade you, am I?

Catherine   No.

Gary   I like you.

Catherine   You what?

Gary   I think you're very energetic.

Catherine   Energetic? Is that the best you can do?

Gary   But I think you should bend your rules about licensing for off-duty coppers.

Catherine   I'm tired.

Gary   I'm thirsty.

Catherine   There's a pub open, up Inverness Street.

Gary   I know.

Catherine   Go there.

Gary   I hate it there.

Catherine   Do you?

Gary   I'll give you a fiver.

Catherine   No.

Gary   I'll give you a lift home.

Catherine   No, Gary, I'm knackered. You should be going home anyway.

Gary   I know.

Catherine   Should go and see your wife.

Gary   I know.

Catherine   So go.

Gary   I will.

Catherine   Now.

Gary   OK.

Catherine   I'll see you tomorrow.

Gary   You really wanna know what I did today?

Catherine   Yeah.

Gary   If I tell you will you get us another beer?

Catherine   Depends what it is.

Gary   Will you?

Catherine   Try us.

Gary   All right. This is what happened to me today:

Marie Louise *addresses the audience.*

Marie Louise   So I'm coming home and I'm walking down the side of the theatre where, where, where *Les Miserables* is playing.

It's maybe eight o'clock at night.

There are people coming home from work, I guess. And other people. Going out. Going out to the theatre. Or the cinema. Or out eating in Chinatown, maybe. Men with taxis. And just by the actual theatre, by the doors at the back, there's a five-year-old child on her own. But it's too dark. It's late. She's too vulnerable to be out here on her own. She can't be. But actually I think she is.

Just near there I see a younger boy holding hands with his mother. He's got this soft blond hair and he's very excited. Stamping his feet up and down like a robot or something. And there are these lights on his trainers which I think, I just think is fantastic.

And down, off, I don't know, Old Compton Street maybe, or one of the streets there, coming up to it I hear the sound of a girl and she's actually, what she's doing is she's screaming. And that seems horrible. But when I get to the alleyway where she is, I see her. She's the same age as the first girl. But what she's doing is she's screaming, just so that she can listen to the sound of the scream reflected on the walls in the alley. Which looks quite fun to me. I almost want to scream too. With her. And everywhere I look I notice all the children. There just seems to be. It's like there are children everywhere.

I get on to Oxford Street, heading up to Oxford Circus and before I get there, I, this is a bit naughty, I decide that I'm going to go into Thornton's, there. I really want to buy some toffee. I just have this this this this urge. So I've decided, really decided, that I'm going to have this toffee. But in the shop, I get there and in the shop they only have diabetic toffee. That's all they have. In the whole shop! So I buy some. And I eat the whole packet. So that I start to feel a bit sick. And when I come out it's like all the children have gone. They've just disappeared. Where can they all of gone? Just like that. It doesn't make any sense. But. I can't see *any*.

I go into Top Shop. I don't buy anything.

And walk past and look up at that church there. In fact, it's not a church, is it? It's a monument.

Beat.

Blackout. Ten seconds.

April

Kentish Town police station. **Gary Burroughs**'s *office. Morning.* **Gary** *and* **Robert** *are working through catalogues of photofit photographs.* **Robert** *pauses in his work. Looks up at* **Gary**. **Gary** *keeps working throughout.*

Robert Nothing?

Gary (*still searching*)   Nothing.

Robert Maybe . . .

Gary What?

Robert Her description was very specific, but . . .

Gary (*trying not to look up from his work*)   But what?

Robert Maybe she was just wrong.

Gary   –

Robert   Maybe she was just fucking cracking up.

Gary   –

Robert   If she was . . .?

Gary (*looking up briefly*)   Yeah?

Robert   Then what have we got?

Gary   Not much.

Robert   No.

They continue working.

How's Dr Schults?

Gary (*turning a page*)   Bearing up.

Robert   Yeah?

Gary *reaches up to get a cigarette without ever letting his eyes leave the page. Has to feel for the cigarette with his fingers.*

Gary   She's very clear-headed. She seems quite . . .

Robert   What?

Gary   She talks a lot of sense.

Robert   Well, she's a teacher, Gary. I should hope she talks a lot of sense.

Gary   I quite like her.

Robert   Oh yeah?

Gary   Not . . . Fucking dick.

Gary *lights his cigarette.*

Robert   How was he this week?

Gary   Quiet.

Robert   Quiet how?

Gary   He cried.

Robert   Right.

Gary (*looking up*)   Are you looking?

Robert (*looking down to photos*)   Course.

Gary   Because if we miss one, Robert . . .

Robert   We won't.

Gary *clears his throat. Turns another page.*

Robert   Our kid's coming down.

Gary   Yeah?

Robert   Going up Centre Point tonight. Play a bit of pool. Should come with us.

Gary   You what?

Robert   Should do.

Gary   –

Robert   I'll be glad just to get out of the house.

Gary   –

Robert   Fucking Esther.

Gary   –

Robert   I said, 'Fucking Esther'.

Gary   What?

Robert   Doing my head in a bit.

Gary   I see.

Robert   She hates it here.

Gary   Does she?

Robert   Keeps going on. Fucking . . . *All* the *time*. About getting stabbed. Getting robbed. Fucking Asian boys on the estate robbing her.

Gary   Did they?

Robert   No.

Gary   –

Robert   Worse back home. Fucking Pakis back home fucking just –

Gary (*looks straight at him*)   Don't.

Robert (*looks straight back*)   What?

Gary   Just don't. Just shut it.

Robert   Just a word. Just a word, Gary.

Pause. They work in silence for a while.

Gary   How you getting on?

Robert   Nowt.

Gary   If we don't find anything, you know what they'll do, don't you?

Robert   Yeah.

Gary   So find something.

Pause. **Gary** *turns another page. Turns it back. Checks a photo and turns the page again.*

Robert   How's Jenny?

Gary   She's all right, thank you.

Robert   Could bring her with yer.

Gary   What?

Robert   If you come out tonight.

Gary   Maybe.

Robert   I'd like to meet her.

Gary   Yeah?

Robert   You never fancied kids?

Gary (*looking up*)   You what?

Robert   I was just wondering if you and Jenny, why you, you know, never had children or owt.

Gary *looks at him for three seconds.*

Robert   Esther's started asking. Reckons it'd be good. Reckons it'd be all right. I don't know what I'd do if she got pregnant. See all this. Wouldn't want to inflict this on anybody. It's not, not, not, just not fair.

Gary   Too expensive.

Robert   Yeah?

Gary   Oh yeah.

Some time. **Robert** *picks up and examines a witness statement, visibly a piece of text rather than a photograph.*

Robert (*savouring the name*)   Marie Louise Burdett. When I went round to her flat. You know those big flats up Kentish Town. The way she looked at us.

Gary   –

Robert   It was weird. Looking at her. Trying to listen to her. Half thinking I want to fuck you.

Gary (*looks up*)   Shouldn't do that.

Robert   What?

Gary   Shouldn't talk about people like that.

Robert   Yer saying you never?

Gary   How old are you again?

Beat. **Gary** *picks up the statement.* **Robert** *rests his feet on the table.* **Gary** *freezes.*

Robert   You found anything?

Gary   No I haven't.

Robert   It's hopeless, Gary. Isn't it?

Gary   What?

Robert   Ten weeks it's been now.

Gary *moves away from him.*

Robert   What are you gonna do?

Gary   I have no idea.

Robert   You gonna come out with us?

Gary   What?

Robert   Tonight, Gary. You coming or what?

Marie Louise *and* **Catherine** *are in a public square in Islington. Lunchtime.* **Catherine** *lies on the ground looking up.* **Marie Louise** *sits on the bench. They are playing a game.*

Marie Louise   In Bloomsbury.

Catherine   Bloomsbury?!?

Marie Louise (*embarrassed*)   Yeah.

Catherine   Wow.

Marie Louise   What?

Catherine   When?

Marie Louise   Nineteen seventy-five.

Catherine   So you're twenty-seven.

Marie Louise (*simultaneously*)   Twenty-six . . . seven. Shit.

Catherine   I'm Nineteen eighty-one. You're six years older than me. (*Beat.*) I have to tell you something.

Marie Louise   What?

Catherine   I . . . It can wait.

Short time.

What was your school like?

Marie Louise   It was. You know, I don't really remember that much about it.

Catherine   No?

Marie Louise   I remember the boys in the year above me.

Catherine   What were they like?

Marie Louise   I thought they were gorgeous. (*Long pause.*) What about you?

Catherine   I remember my friend Lucy, all her toys, how they were better than mine. And I remember going round to her house and eating peanuts and ice cream. And the smell of grass at school. And I had this Barbie doll with this metallic dress that was the coolest thing I ever saw.

Short time.

I can't stop thinking about that girl.

Marie Louise   No.

Catherine   How long has it been now?

Marie Louise   Three months.

Catherine   Last week, I just went out, I bought a coat. A hundred pound coat. Just to get my mind . . . I don't have a hundred pounds.

Marie Louise   No.

They spend some time soaking in the sun. Then **Catherine** *props herself up on her elbows. Looks up at* **Marie Louise***.*

Catherine   This is good.

Marie Louise   What?

Catherine   This. It's nice.

Marie Louise   Yes. It is.

Catherine   We should do this more often.

Marie Louise   We should.

Catherine (*sitting up*)   What was your mum like?

Marie Louise   She was very beautiful.

Catherine   I bet she was.

Marie Louise   Why?

Catherine   Because I think you are too.

Marie Louise   She used to be a model. And a painter.

Catherine   Did she?

Marie Louise   She sat, actually, one time, this is the truth, she sat for David Hockney.

Catherine   What about your dad?

Marie Louise   He's . . . He's always wringing his hands. I hate that.

Catherine (*going to sit with her*)   And do you prefer cats or dogs?

Marie Louise   Cats.

Catherine   And what's your favourite clothing?

Marie Louise   Anything cashmere.

Catherine   Get you!

Marie Louise   What!?!

Catherine   What kind of music do you like?

Marie Louise   Jazz. Jazzy. Jazz music.

Catherine (*looking straight at her*)   And have you ever been in love?

Marie Louise (*looking out*)   Yes.

Catherine   Have you?

Marie Louise   Yes.

Catherine   Who with?

Marie Louise   With my last boyfriend.

Catherine   What was he called?

Marie Louise   Steven.

Catherine (*pushing herself forward with the balls of both hands*) And what happened to Steven?

Marie Louise   It didn't work out.

Catherine   Why?

Marie Louise   Cause he was just –

Catherine   What?

Marie Louise   Nothing.

Silence. **Catherine** *looks out too.*

Marie Louise   I want my mum to leave my dad.

Silence.

Actually I want him to die.

They laugh together. Pause.

Catherine   I love my parents, me. (*Beat.*) Marie Louise.

Marie Louise (*turns to her*)   Do you want kids?

Catherine   You what?

Marie Louise   Do you, Catherine?

Catherine   Yes.

Marie Louise   Do you?

Catherine   Definitely.

Marie Louise   I think you'd be a good mother.

Catherine   I think I'd be a GREAT mother. Yeah. (*Beat.*) Marie Louise.

Marie Louise   I think you're . . .

Catherine   What?

Marie Louise   You're very, stylish. You have a great style.

Catherine   I want to tell you something.

Marie Louise   Do you know what frightens me?

Catherine   What?

Marie Louise   You'll think I'm very strange.

Catherine   What?

Marie Louise   I'm frightened that I'm going to live too long.

Long pause.

What was it that you wanted to tell me?

Catherine   Marie Louise I can't pay my rent this month.

Panatica's café. Afternoon. **Gary** *is drinking coffee. He is on his feet. Pacing.* **Catherine** *is working. She is pouring salt from a large bottle into individual table salt cellars. He doesn't look at her when he talks to her. Looks out of the windows, out of the door, at the floor, into his coffee cup, anywhere but at her.*

Gary   You should leave.

Catherine   You don't know what you're talking about.

Gary   I do.

Catherine   I need the money.

Gary   That's a bullshit excuse.

Catherine   No it isn't, Gary. What is it with you today?

Gary   There are plenty of jobs better, more interesting, more demanding, more . . . you're just –

Catherine   I like it.

Gary   No you don't.

Catherine   I like the punters. I like the conversation. I like you normally. Unless you're being –

Gary   And what about fat twat?

Catherine   I hate him but –

Gary   You see.

Catherine   Everybody hates their boss.

Gary   I don't hate my boss.

Catherine   That's different.

Gary   Why?

Catherine   Cause your job is your career.

Gary   My career?

Catherine   What you are. Your job is what you are. But this is a just a way –

Gary   What are you going on about?

Catherine   Just a way of paying for me to get myself through college. I need it. I won't be doing it for ever.

Gary   I just think you're worth more than this.

Catherine   I am. I am worth more than this.

Gary   I was so glad to get out. Me. Of Brum. Just go.

Beat. He stands still. Puts his coffee down. Flexes and unflexes his fingers. Looks at her.

Can I have a beer please?

Catherine   You told me not to serve you any beer.

Gary   I know.

Catherine   You told me not to.

Gary   I changed my mind.

Catherine   Have you finished work yet?

Gary   Yes.

Catherine   Have you really?

Gary   Yes.

Catherine   You haven't, have you?

Gary   No.

Catherine   It's a contravention of my licence to serve an on-duty policeman.

Gary   I know that! I won't *nick* you!

Catherine   I'll get you a coffee.

Gary (*moving in on her*)   I *want* a *beer*.

Catherine   Gary. No.

Gary   You think I can't . . . I've been drinking since I was thirteen. I've been smoking since I was eleven.

Catherine   What's that got to do with anything?

Gary (*raising his fist above the back of his head*)   It's just fucking ridiculous, Catherine, honestly, mate. It's fucking –

Catherine   Gary, don't talk to me like that.

Gary   If you knew what I had to do this afternoon!

Catherine   What?

No response.

What do you mean?

Some time. **Gary** *tries to calm down. Inhales and exhales through his teeth.* **Catherine** *puts the bottle away and starts screwing the tops on the cellars.* **Gary** *turns away from her again, wrestles with the change in his pockets.*

Gary   How's your new house?

Catherine   Arright.

Gary   And the new flatmate?

Catherine   She's arright. Bit.

Gary   What?

Catherine   She's very as mad as a fucking hat. But she's all right. Harmless you know? Rent's cheap.

Gary (*slight laugh*)   That's good.

Catherine   Croydon's just the same, you know.

Gary   What?

Catherine (*while she talks,* **Gary** *nods*)   No different to Birmingham. Just shit. Everything. Hate it. Better up here.

Gary (*turns to look at her*)   You think so?

Catherine   At least there's things to do.

Gary   Yeah.

Beat. They look at each other.

Robert *addresses the audience.*

Robert   I leave my house and I'm heading for the tube.

It's dark.

I can hear some music coming from somewhere behind me and to my left.

I'm aware that I'm walking much slower than I ordinarily would have done.

And I turn the corner, change direction and the music seems to be still coming from behind me. Still to me left. And and and I'm counting the uncracked paving stones. And there seems to be just hundreds of them.

Underneath the railway tracks at Kentish Town West a train goes past and I just think, how much I want to be asleep on a train. How good that would feel. Actually. Right now.

And the light is dimming.

And it's getting cold.

And just turning before Kentish Town Road there's a park, a kiddies' playground, bits of grass, all that and there is litter, strewn all over it. Cans and waste paper and sweet wrappers and bottles. And it seems, to me, it seems just plain shameful. That people should do that. They should concrete the lot. I mean, why bother? They should just cover it up.

West of Kentish Town Road there are cranes putting together a block of flats or offices or something. I love the way that cranes look in the nights. Like birds. Like huge spiders. And I want to, just to climb up it. Nobody would see us. Nobody would stop us. Nobody would do owt. And the things you could see. It would be just magnificent.

And the music's getting louder which doesn't make sense. But I can't quite distinguish it. And it's still coming from behind me and still coming from the left.

I turn up the main road heading towards the pedestrian crossing and for the first time I remember where I am. Exactly where I am. And there's the yellow and the red and the light of McDonald's and I'm so happy to see it. To know that it is there. That it remains there. It looks like a beacon. Like a big old glow. And I cross the pedestrian crossing. And I'm in the tube station. With the floor wet and cold and the wind and the noise and the smell of a tube station, the smell that tube stations always have. And I go straight down.

Kentish Town police station. **Gary Burroughs**'s *office. Early evening.* **Marie Louise** *sits with her hands folded on her lap.*

Gary *sits opposite her. He has a pen in his hand, a folder open in front of him.*

Marie Louise   I don't believe this. I don't believe that nothing has been, can be, has been done.

Gary   Miss Burdett. There are some details I need to check.

Marie Louise   I really. I don't. Can I speak to your supervising officer please?

Gary   I need to clarify some of the things which you told my colleague.

Marie Louise   It's been months and months. You're doing nothing.

Gary   There are some elements of your statement you might wish to clarify.

Marie Louise   To *clarify*? I'd like to speak to your supervising officer please.

Gary   That may not be necessary. You told my colleague DC Evans that you saw a girl that you thought resembled Daisy Schults in the Seven Dials area of Covent Garden two days prior to your interview on the 23rd of January this year, is that correct?

Marie Louise   I think so.

Gary   You think so?

Marie Louise   Yes it is. It is correct.

Gary   That she was wearing a red coat. That her hair was tied back. These were details that you recognised from the family photograph broadcast shortly before you contacted the police. That you were surprised because she seemed to be in a state of some distress and that she was being forced north across the Seven Dials by a man that you describe as being a black-haired Caucasian aged perhaps forty, slightly overweight. Is *that* correct?

Marie Louise   That's correct. That's all correct.

Gary   This is the statement that you are intent on pursuing?

Marie Louise   I want to know why nothing has been done about what I saw.

Gary   You claim, and I quote from your statement: 'Two nights ago. Maybe about six o'clock.' And then when asked why you didn't contact the police immediately, you said, and again I quote: 'I waited a day to be sure it was her.'

Marie Louise   Yes.

Gary   Miss Burdett. That would have timed your sighting of her at six o'clock on Sunday the 21st.

Marie Louise   This is absurd.

Gary   The photograph wasn't broadcast until the ten o'clock news, Miss Burdett.

Marie Louise   –

Gary   You couldn't have seen the photograph before the time you saw the girl that you recognised as Daisy, Miss Burdett. Nobody could have done.

Marie Louise   –

Gary   You know it wasn't her, don't you, Miss Burdett?

Marie Louise   I might have got the time wrong.

Gary   You were clear and specific at the time of your interview.

Marie Louise   I might have done. People make mistakes.

Gary   When you were questioned you repeated the same details over, on two occasions.

Pause. **Gary** *looks at her. She looks away.*

Marie Louise   Can I have a glass of water please?

Gary   It happens all the time. People see, they think they see things. They want to see things. It's like they see phantoms of –

Marie Louise   It wasn't a phantom.

Gary   We don't charge them normally. We could. Wasting police time.

Marie Louise   I saw her.

Gary   Miss Burdett, we decided not to pursue this line of inquiry.

Pause. **Gary** *gathers papers.*

Marie Louise   I don't know what to say.

Gary (*standing*)   Thank you for your concern. I understand your anxiety. It must have felt as though we were wilfully neglecting your statement. I can assure you that wasn't the case. I want to thank you for your time.

Marie Louise   I don't know what to do.

Beat. He touches her hand.

Gary   I understand, y'know? I do. People get . . .

Late afternoon. Alone at first, **Anne** *waits at home for the expected arrival of* **Gary** *and* **Robert**. *They arrive after a few moments. They are wearing coats. She welcomes them.*

Anne (*standing*)   Hello. Hello. Come in. Come in. Just, just, just, can I take your coats?

Robert   Thank you.

Gary   Thank you.

They take their coats off. Remain standing. She hangs their coats up. Comes back. Folds her arms.

Anne   Please. Sit. Sit. Sit down. Just. How are you both?

Gary   We're all right. Yeah.

They sit.

Robert   Yeah. Fine.

Anne   Good. Good. That's good. That's . . . Can I get you anything? Please. A cup of tea. Or, or, or coffee.

Gary   We –

Anne   Please.

Gary   A coffee would be lovely.

Robert   Yes. For me as well.

Anne   Good. Coffee. How would you like it?

Gary   Black, no sugar.

Robert   Milk, one. Please.

Anne   Right. Good. Just. Wait here.

She leaves them. They both sit down. Still for some time. **Gary** *turns his mobile phone off.* **Robert** *stares at the floor.*

Anne (*off*)   It looks like it's going to be a beautiful day tomorrow. They said. I saw.

Gary   Yeah. I saw that.

Anne (*off*)   We, me and and and John we might go out to the countryside, if it stays good at the weekend.

Gary   Oh yeah?

She comes back in with a tray of coffee and biscuits.

Anne   Go down to Sussex. Maybe Brighton. Here you are.

Gary   Lovely.

Anne   I brought you some biscuits. Have a biscuit.

Gary (*taking one*)   Thank you.

Robert (*taking one*)   Thank you.

They put their biscuits down and don't touch them again.

Gary   How is Mr Petrie?

Anne   He's all right. Yes. He's all right.

Gary   Good (*Beat.*) Dr Schults –

Anne   Anne.

Gary   Anne. We've got some news.

Anne   Right. Right. Right. Right. Right.

Gary   Would you like to sit down?

Anne   No no no I'll stand.

Gary   Anne, the investigation, as you know, the investigation has been proceeding for ten weeks now.

Anne   Yes.

Gary   There's been no real progress.

Anne   No.

Gary   The description we were given matched nothing that we have on our records. It led nowhere.

Anne   No. You said. It wasn't. Necessarily. It could have been a perfectly . . .

Gary   Yes.

Beat.

At a meeting this morning a decision was made regarding the search for Daisy. It has been decided that the evidence that we have on the case does not warrant the level of manpower currently being expended in the investigation. We remain too unconfident about specific elements. The details of her activities. The details of her appearance. Her knowledge of the environment. We have found no clues. No developments have been made. At present we have ten officers working on the investigation full-time and a reserve staff of fifty officers pursuing the investigation on at least a part-time basis. It has been decided that eight of the remaining ten officers involved in the search for Daisy will be moved away from working exclusively on the case and that the fifty officers in reserve will be returned to their regular duties. This will leave two officers involved exclusively in her search, representing the Missing Persons Division but working for the Child Protection Team. These will be myself and Detective Constable Evans, Robert.

Anne   Right.

Gary   We have also decided upon a new tactic in proceeding with the investigation. We have decided to scale down the geographical area in which we are going to be searching. We've decided to concentrate on a much more thorough investigation of the north London area.

Anne   What do you mean?

Gary   We are set to embark on a very thorough and comprehensive series of interviews with all residents of north London currently recorded on the national register.

Anne   You're going to . . .

Gary   A series of interviews that will in time move away from the north London area and take in all of central and then greater London.

Silence.

Do you understand what I have told you?

Silence.

Anne   Doesn't it warrant more officers? Gary, if, if, if you've found nothing. Gary. If you've found nothing then doesn't it make more sense to employ more officers rather than, rather than, rather than less? I mean, it sounds like you're giving up!

Gary   Dr Schults, in cases like this case, sometimes a more concentrated –

Anne   Hasn't the register been checked already? Gary?

Gary   There's a difference between an inquiry and an interview –

Anne   Do you think she's been taken now?

Gary   I'm afraid we have to consider that as a possibility.

She looks at him for a long time.

Anne   What do you *think*?

Gary   I don't know.

Anne   No, I know that but but but what do you *think*?

Gary   I really can't say. I just don't know.

Anne   And if she has been it's very likely that she's been killed, isn't it?

Gary   I couldn't say.

Anne   But she probably has been, hasn't she?

Gary   I don't know.

Anne   She can't have been gone for for for so long. Nobody could have taken her for so long, for that, and kept her alive, could they?

Gary   We can't possibly tell at this stage.

Anne   Does that happen ever?

Gary   We couldn't say at this stage.

Anne   I'm asking you if that happens ever?

Gary   It's very, very unusual.

Anne   But it happens. It has happened.

Gary   Yes. It has happened.

Anne   Have you know it happen?

Gary   I –

Anne Have you investigated a case in which it has happened? Gary, have you?

No response. He looks down.

Oh Christ, God.

She sits and cries. Bites her fist. Her shoulders shaking.

Gary Can I get you anything? (*To* **Robert**.) Some water.

Robert *fetches water.* **Gary** *stands to touch her back. Doesn't.*

Gary Anne, I swear to you we will try, with everything that we have, with *everything* to find her. (*Pause.*) Is there anything which you are unclear about? Anything at all.

Anne (*arms wrapped around herself, looking up*) No. No. No. I don't think so.

Robert *returns.*

Gary There is still the option of employing a full-time Family Liaison Officer –

Anne No.

Gary Anne, after we've left, this afternoon, or tonight if you have any questions about this. About anything regarding this or about anything, ring me. You can ring me at the office or on the office mobile, or here, this is my personal mobile. Any time. Day or night. Don't even hesitate. Do you promise me?

Anne I –

Gary Anne.

Anne Yes. I promise.

Robert What time is Mr Schults coming home?

Anne It's Mr Petrie. My husband's name is Petrie.

Catherine *addresses the audience.*

Catherine   I'm heading east.

Out towards the City.

There's this man on the Central Line. And when I see him for the first time he looks quite together. But I'm drawn back to him. To looking at him. He can't hold my eye contact. And as I look at him I notice that his fingernails are dusty. And that his raincoat is old and dusty too. And he is unshaven. And his hair is cut badly. And that there are cuts on his face.

The floor of the tube train is spattered with phlegm. And it is men who have spat there.

There's this boy, he must be maybe thirteen years old and he is too exhausted even to hold his head up.

And I can smell rubber and after-shave.

And when the train pulls into the station the screech of the brakes is horrible. Horrible. And I can't believe that nobody else notices. And I'm not sure but I think that the man I saw on the train gets off at the same station as me.

And there is flute music in the station, echoing down the corridors and the sound of the lift-doors-closing alarm.

In my mouth I can taste Red Bull and chocolate.

And outside on Cheapside there is a crane, towering above me, and it's horrible. And the sound of slaughtering metal. And the cars are being shaken by the bass tubes. And the men inside them. Physically shaken. You can watch them. And feel it in your feet. And the men's voices outside the bars there are the same. They are all drinking outside in their, in their, in their suits and their voices have, they have the same violence.

I look round to see if he's been following me because I sensed something, I sensed something I sensed a, a, a, a. But there's nobody there.

And the doors on the bars look like they want to crush you.

And there are no stars in the sky.

And I can't find the moon.

Blackout. Ten seconds.

August

Night-time. **Robert** *is drinking in the Centre Point pool hall. At the table there.* **Gary** *has found him.* **Robert** *is drunk. Holding a pool cue. He holds it like a weapon almost. There is a long pause before they speak. Looking straight at one another.* **Gary** *holds his hand up, as though warning him or calming him.*

Robert   Your fault this.

Gary   Robert.

Pause.

Robert (*breathing hard*)   Sometimes I want to kill you.

Gary   What?

Robert   Should have got him.

Gary   I –

Robert   Should have gone in. Should have done, done, done, done *something*.

Gary   Robert, please, keep your voice –

Robert (*as though straining to keep quiet*)   I wanted to and you *stopped* me. *You stopped me.* And it was wrong and you should start to think about how you are going to take responsibility for that, Gary, because it was your fault.

Gary   Robert, listen.

Robert   With your stubborn fucking patronising fucking . . .

Robert *raises the cue slightly.*

Gary   –

Robert   I hate it. I hate the way you fucking look at me
sometimes. And the way you fucking talk to me. And talk
about me. And the way you never listen to a fucking
word I say but you just fucking just always just don't say
nothing. I hate it.

Pause.

And I hate the way you eat.

Gary   Robert, calm –

Robert *looks around himself as though checking other people's
reactions to his anger. He is straining to hold his voice down.*

Robert   Don't tell me to calm down! For fuck's sake!
Coming down here! Telling me! How fucking dare you?
How fucking dare you do that?

Gary   I had something to tell –

Robert   Honestly, Gary, fucking don't.

Pause. **Gary** *lets him settle and stew.* **Robert** *turns away, lowers
his cue.*

This place! It's fucking crackers! It does my head in. It
makes me want to just fucking –

He becomes still.

I go home at night and just the sound now of the way that
Esther has started to breathe even makes me fucking want
to tear out my teeth. And it's your fault.

Long pause. He stares at **Gary** *who stands still.*

She keeps going on.

Gary   Robert, something's –

Robert   I'm going, me. I'm gonna fuck off. Fuck off back
up home. Fuck this. Fuck this job. Fucking – Fuck you. Fuck
you. Fuck you. Fuck her. Fuck her kid. Fuck 'em all.

Robert *lets the cue drop to the floor.*

Gary   Robert, they've found a body.

Robert   They what?

Gary   Just heard. This evening. Some woman. On the north bank of the Thames. Low tide. Just west of Millbank. Opposite MI5. It's a little girl.

Robert   Right.

Gary   We're going in to see it first thing tomorrow.

Long pause. **Robert** *looks away from* **Gary** *for three seconds and then looks back at his chin.*

Robert   Not everybody likes you, y'know.

Gary   You what?

Robert   You think they do but you're fucking wrong. Not everybody does.

Gary   You swear too much. You shouldn't swear as much as you do. There's no need for it. Tomorrow morning, you better be ready.

Panatica's café. Night. **Gary** *is drinking with* **Catherine**. *Looking largely at their drinks.*

Catherine   You're very quiet.

Gary   What?

Catherine   Tonight.

Gary   Am I?

Catherine   Bad day?

Gary   No no no no. It was all right. It was, yeah. It was good. It was fine.

Catherine   We've been dead.

Gary Yeah?

Catherine Too hot to work.

Gary I know that feeling.

Catherine Too hot to do anything. I hate it here when it's hot.

Gary How come?

Catherine It gets so grimy. Sorry. I shouldn't be telling you this, should I. But it does.

Gary It's all right. I don't really eat here.

Catherine If you did I'd tell you not to.

Gary Why?

Catherine The kitchen here. Makes you sick.

Gary Does it?

Catherine He wants locking up. I'll tell you that for nothing. If anybody does he does. Fat cunt.

Pause. He looks straight at her.

Gary I wish . . .

Catherine What?

Gary *smiles, pulls a cigarette out. Doesn't light it.*

Gary I like talking to you.

Catherine Good.

Gary I wish you didn't always just make me leave all the time.

Catherine I wish you'd let me go home on time. Get some kip. Yer with me?

Gary Can I ask you something?

Catherine Go on.

Gary   Would you want to be a mother ever? If you had the chance.

Catherine   Damn right I would.

Gary   Would you?

Catherine   Yeah. Duurr.

Gary   What?

Catherine   Course I would.

Gary   That's good.

Catherine   I'd be a great mum, me and all.

Gary   Would you?

Catherine   Yeah.

Gary   How's that?

Catherine   What do you mean?

Gary   What would make you a good mum, do you think?

Catherine   I'd be very patient. I'd be very generous. I'd be very loving.

Gary *puts his cigarette in his mouth.*

Gary   Yeah.

Catherine   Yeah what?

Gary   I think you would. I think you're right.

Gary *lights a match. Lets it burn for a bit. Shakes it out. Takes his cigarette out of his mouth and puts it back in the packet.*

Catherine   What you asking that for?

Gary   Just . . .

Pause.

He looks away for some time, drinks, wipes his mouth with the back of his hand and then looks straight back at her.

Do you know something?

Catherine   What?

Gary   I think you're lovely.

Long pause.

People should know things like that about themselves. I think. I think not enough people tell each other things like that and they should and I wanted to tell you.

Catherine   Thank you.

Gary   I had this thing.

Catherine   What?

Gary   When I was younger, I used to go and look at galleries. Just look at pictures. Go to the National Gallery. Or the National Portrait Gallery or some of the smaller ones. I used to like looking at the pictures. Sometimes in the middle of the day when I was working I'd do it. Just go and I was thinking. I can't.

Catherine   What?

Gary   This is going to sound really stupid actually.

Catherine   What?

Gary   I would have liked to take you to one of these galleries. Go with you. Just go and look at some pictures. But I can't. It'd be. I just – There's no way.

Long pause.

Catherine   No.

Gary   Just . . . stupid. I'm sorry.

Morning. Harvey Nichols. The café in the food hall on the fifth floor. A beautiful new morning. Big, big presence of sunshine. **Marie Louise** *and* **Catherine**. *Long pause.* **Marie Louise** *looks out of the window. And then looks straight at* **Catherine**.

Marie Louise   I wanted to ask you something.

Catherine   What?

Marie Louise   I might not though.

Catherine   What?

Marie Louise   No. I think I won't.

Catherine   What?

Marie Louise   It's so bright! God!

Catherine   –

Marie Louise   You know you said you really want to have a baby.

Catherine   Yeah.

Marie Louise   I've been thinking about this all morning. Since they found that girl. And what I thought was that actually, I'm terrified of babies. I am. They, they, they, they scare me.

Catherine   It must have been –

Marie Louise   Just the feeling of them.

Catherine   Don't you –

Marie Louise (*looking out, maybe shading her eyes*)   I like it here. I think this view is my favourite view over the city. The gardens. All of the high street.

Catherine   Good hot chocolate.

Marie Louise (*looking back briefly*)   Good what?

Catherine   This hot chocolate. It's very chocolatey. Very thick.

Marie Louise   It's such a beautiful morning.

Catherine   Yeah.

Marie Louise   I love summer in England. A really good summer's day. You don't get them very often.

Long pause. **Catherine** *stirs her hot chocolate. The spoon rattling around the sides of the cup. She goes to raise it to her mouth.*

Marie Louise (*looking back*)   Do you miss having a man around?

Catherine   No.

Marie Louise   No, me neither.

Catherine   I should hope not.

Marie Louise   I think I'm doing fine. I think it's great. It's good. I like it. Better off without them.

Marie Louise   Have you ever done anything stupid? I mean really stupid and terrible.

Catherine   –

Marie Louise   One time I told something to the police and it wasn't true. Is that, do you think that's awful?

Catherine   It depends what –

Marie Louise   I thought, I really thought that I saw this thing once. (*Beat.*) Just a child, she was, just, smiling. And now I don't think that I did.

Beat. **Catherine** *stares at her.* **Marie Louise** *looks away.*

Catherine   Marie Louise –

Marie Louise   There are so many things I'm going to do this next six months. Before the end of the year . . .

Catherine   What like?

Marie Louise   I'm going to sing.

Catherine   You sing all the time.

Marie Louise   No, but really sing. Take it seriously.

Catherine   I think that's –

Marie Louise   And I'm going to start writing.

Catherine   Writing?

Marie Louise   Just writing things down. Maybe try to send some things in somewhere. It's all about –

Catherine   What?

Marie Louise   Indelibility. To indelibly leave my thumbprint. So that it's like you're not even dead. Should we get a cat?

Catherine   A cat.

Marie Louise   I always wanted to get a cat but I don't think we should now. Catherine, I heard what you did.

Catherine   What?

Marie Louise   I heard what you did to me.

Catherine   What?

Marie Louise   Just. Don't.

Catherine   Marie Louise, I don't know what you're talking about.

Marie Louise   Sometimes I want to get all my hair and just cut it all off.

Catherine   What?

Marie Louise   Out on Kentish Town high street. Coming home. This homeless guy. He had no shoes on. There was blood on his feet. Nobody stopped actually.

Catherine   –

Marie Louise   Sometimes I want to get all my hair and just cut it all off. Do you ever get like that?

Catherine   Sometimes.

Marie Louise   And and and washing up! Because let's face it. With you. I could just open the window, yeah, and just throw them all away and buy a whole new big load of plates.

Catherine Have I done something to upset you, Marie Louise –

Marie Louise To 'upset' me?

Catherine Because if I have –

Marie Louise No, not 'upset'. Not 'upset'.

Catherine I really don't know what it is and I –

Marie Louise Let's just not. Talk about it. It's better not to. It's just something I heard. Might not even be true.

Catherine If you'd tell me.

Marie Louise I have had such a . . . I didn't sleep.

Catherine –

Marie Louise I can't stop thinking about it.

Catherine No. Me neither.

Marie Louise Twenty-eight weeks. Can you imagine it, Catherine? The poor, poor, poor, little. I hope you don't take this the wrong way, and I'm sure it must be complicated with, because I have a certain position and a certain amount of, well, money, but I think that you have, sometimes I think this, you have the capacity actually to exploit people and if I had to say one thing that I didn't like about you it would be that.

Catherine Fucking hell.

Marie Louise Don't swear.

Catherine What?

Marie Louise You swear all the time.

Pause.

Look!

Catherine   What?

Marie Louise   Out there!

Catherine   What?

Marie Louise   You can see the Wheel!

Anne Schults's *house. Morning.* **Gary** *and* **Anne**. *She has stopped crying.*

Anne   What time is it?

Gary   It's eleven o'clock.

Anne   What am I going to do?

Gary   –

Anne   What am I going to do, Gary?

Gary   I –

Anne   Where's Robert?

Gary   At the station.

Anne   You need to go, don't you?

Gary   No.

Anne   What am I going to . . .? I've got to go to Sainsbury's. I need to buy some food.

Gary   I could –

Anne   No. I want to. And I'll stop at the post office. There's something I should . . .

She turns away suddenly, perhaps catches her breath.

Gary   What?

Anne   I'm going to have to ring people. Or write to them.

Gary   Yes.

Anne   And talk to the, the, the radio people. All that.

Gary We can help you with that.

Anne I won't do an interview.

Gary No.

Anne We were going to go away! Me and John! Go to France! Can you imagine?

Gary You could still . . .

Anne But all of the things, we need to arrange things. And invite people. There are people we want to to to see. What am I going to do?

Gary –

Anne I'll have to sort out her bedroom. All her things.

Gary If there's –

Anne I'm going to go to the chemist. And I'm going to clean the kitchen. And sort out all of the jars of food. Check their sell-by dates. And clean the bathroom. I'm going to go to his work. I'm going to find him and tell him.

Blackout. One minute.

November

Gary *addresses the audience.*

Gary I'm heading down Charing Cross Road towards Embankment. It's just starting to get dark. There are one or two people just starting to finish work.

There are two children's toys, two toy bikes just parked, parked by this tree by the side of the pub there . . . All the plastic is blue and yellow, trashy. And I find it really irritating that somebody has just left these things there. And now with all these people, everybody just, just walking past them. Like they don't give all that much.

I really want to get a drink.

There are these two homeless people on Embankment. They're juggling. One of them is. Just juggling these two poxy little batons, and his mate, who's younger than him, has a hat with a little sign on and when I walk past them they don't ask me or nothing but the way they look at me, particularly that cunt with the sign, the young fucker, the way he looks at me. Because I don't give them any money or anything. Makes me want. How dare you make me feel like that for what you're doing after all the things I've done in my day.

I want to beat the shit out of them.

I can taste bitter and tobacco in my mouth.

I cross the bridge. Cross Hungerford Bridge. By this time it's getting to be near enough five thirty. Stood over the water. Looking through the metal slats at the river below. It's like, for a second, it honestly sounds like the river has started to roar. It looks, it just looks indomitable. And there's something so truthful about that. That it has been there for so long. And that it will survive me and survive all this. I feel like it justifies me. That I am justified. Just because of the size of the river. And the history. And it's getting cold but that knowledge feels good. It feels important to know this.

And I get to the station.

I'm tired.

And I'm getting hungry.

And all I want to do is go home and go to bed with someone.

Outside **Marie Louise**'s *flat. Late afternoon.* **Catherine** *is leaving. They wear coats.* **Marie Louise** *hugs her arms around herself.* **Catherine** *has a bag at her feet.*

Marie Louise   Have you got everything?

Catherine   Yeah.

Marie Louise   If you've left anything I'll just –

Catherine   Sure.

Marie Louise   – give you a ring and you can . . . Or I can send it to you.

Catherine   That would be –

Catherine *goes to pick up her bag.*

Marie Louise   I'm sorry.

Catherine (*stops*)   What for?

Marie Louise   For, y'know.

Catherine   Really. Don't be.

Marie Louise   I just get.

Catherine (*picks the bag up*)   I know.

Marie Louise   Sometimes.

Catherine (*swings it on to her shoulder*)   I'm exactly the same.

Marie Louise   Yeah. (*Looks up.*) The moon's out.

Catherine (*sees it*)   Early.

Marie Louise   I like that. This time of year.

Catherine (*turning to move away*)   Yeah.

Marie Louise   I'd love to go to the moon, me. One day. Look down on stuff.

Catherine (*looks at her for a while*)   I –

Marie Louise   Actually, you know what I'd love to do.

Catherine   What?

Marie Louise   I'd love to travel more. Spend some time. Take some time off. Go everywhere.

Catherine   Everywhere?

Marie Louise   All over the world.

Catherine (*smiling*)   You could probably afford that,
couldn't you?

Marie Louise   What do you mean?

Catherine   Nothing, I just –

Marie Louise   What would you do?

Catherine   What?

Marie Louise   If you took time off? A whole, you know.

Catherine   I don't know.

Marie Louise   I'd love to read more. Just. Or study. I
made such a mess of my, my, my . . . If I regretted anything
I think it would be that.

Catherine *smiles. Looks away.*

Catherine   Yeah.

Marie Louise   How are you getting there?

Catherine   Go on the tube. Just a couple of stops.

Marie Louise   I could get you a taxi or something.

Catherine   No, it's nothing.

Marie Louise   And it's funny.

Catherine   What?

Marie Louise   Because I won't study. Or this whole, this
writing thing. That won't happen. Or the singing.

Pause. **Catherine** *looks at her.*

Do you know what I mean?

Catherine   Yeah.

Marie Louise   It won't, that won't. Which is a shame. I
think. I wish you so much luck.

Catherine   Thank you.

Marie Louise   I so love the way you're, you get, you have this this passion.

Catherine   Thank you.

Marie Louise   And, in the future, if you had a child. Would you rather have a son or a daughter?

Catherine   A daughter, I think.

Marie Louise   I hope that you get a daughter then.

Catherine   One day.

Marie Louise   Yes. I know I must have let you down.

Catherine   –

Marie Louise   It's just . . . Do you know?

Catherine   What?

Marie Louise   I'd really, one day. I'd love to go back to Bloomsbury. Go back and live there. I'd love that. Just pack everything up into my boxes and my bags and just jolly well just go go go home.

Catherine   Would you?

Marie Louise (*looking away*)   I'd love that. I would just, just love it. I –

Catherine   You should calm down sometimes.

Marie Louise   What?

Catherine   Not get so nervous about things.

Marie Louise   No.

Catherine   Because. I think. You're very frank.

Marie Louise   Frank.

Catherine   And that's good.

Marie Louise   Thank you.

Catherine   Just . . .

Marie Louise   What?

Catherine   Nothing. Here.

They go to hug but **Catherine***'s bag makes it awkward, clumsy, shit.*

I'll see you soon, Marie Louise.

Marie Louise   You promise?

Regent's Park. Morning. Within sight of the jackals' enclosure at London Zoo. **Anne** *and* **Robert** *stand looking at them. They don't look at each other while they talk.*

Beat. About the jackals.

Anne   He looks bored.

Robert   Keeps scratching.

Anne   Are you cold?

Robert   No. No. I'm fine. Are you all right?

Anne   Yes. Thank you.

Beat. She looks at him briefly then away again.

Funny coming here. I've not been here for ages. It was good of you two to come all this way. There was something I – (*smiling.*) I'm so odd sometimes. I'm sorry.

Robert   No. Really. Don't be sorry. God.

Anne   It's just the house is a bit of a mess. I was trying to think of somewhere and I remembered this place and I just thought. Silly.

Robert   I like it. I've never been here before.

Pause.

I like zoos. Looking at all the animals.

Pause.

The way they look at you. This way you don't even have to pay.

Anne (*smiles at him*)   How's Gary treating you?

Robert   All right. Yeah. Not bad.

Anne   How's Gary treating himself?

Robert   What do –

Anne   He smokes too much. Drinks too much. It's stupid.

Robert   He's. You know.

Gary *enters with three cups.*

Gary   One tea (**Anne**'s), one coffee white (**Robert**'s) and one coffee black (*his own*).

Some time. Looking at the enclosure.

I like jackals.

Some more.

So. Brighton.

Anne   Yeah.

Gary   When?

Anne   About three weeks.

Gary   That'll be good. Yer know. Sea and that. Be beautiful.

Anne   I hope so.

Gary   No, I do. I think it's a really good idea.

Anne   I just wanted to see you. To let you know.

Gary   Yeah. That's good of you. Means a lot to us.

Robert   Yeah.

Anne   We got your flowers. They were lovely. Thank you.

Gary   That's all right.

Anne   She'd have been twelve. Funny. And then soon it's Christmas. And it won't be long now until it's a year. And that's another anniversary. Isn't it?

They drink their drinks.

I'm sure that one's looking at me.

They smile.

Robert   You gonna carry on teaching?

Anne   I think so. There's a post coming up, at the University of Sussex.

Robert   Oh yeah?

Anne   Yeah. But –

Robert   What?

Anne   Institutions. Sometimes, you know the song 'Heroes' by David Bowie?

Robert   Yeah.

Anne   When I was a kid that was my favourite song. I used to love David Bowie. Sometimes. In the Senior Common Room. I just want to stand on a table and just sing it. Up at the top of my voice.

Smiles. Some time.

Gary   How's Mr Petrie?

Anne   He's all right. He had an affair.

Gary   –

Anne   Just a. Nothing serious. It's over now. We're doing all right. Eat a lot of fish and chips together. Watch a lot of television. He's still teaching. He's got a job in the, the media department. (*Pause.*) I used to think he was so beautiful. A little bit fat but – I used to love his eyes and the way he was so intelligent. Making a house for him.

Gary Are you all right?

Anne I'm fine. Yeah. Yes. Yes. I'm good.

Gary We need to be going soon.

Anne I used to come here with Billy Franks.

Gary Who was Billy Franks?

Anne Billy Franks was the first boy I ever kissed. When I was a girl. We used to come here at break times. I went to school just up in Camden. Come down to the zoo. I remember the first time I kissed him. How it felt. How soft his lips felt. Could be . . . And I split up with him. I ditched him. And made him cry. I'm telling him that I don't want to go out with him any more and he just starts crying. He's fourteen. Never saw him much after that. Never saw him at all after I left school. Wonder what he's doing now. I'd love to, just, to see him. Tell him I'm sorry.

Pause. The three stare out. Drink their tea and coffee.

Anne Do you think we're getting old, Gary?

Gary Yeah.

Anne Does it bother you?

Gary I don't think about it.

Some time.

Anne There was – I wanted to – I bought a present for the two of you. But I left it at home. I decided not to. I'm going to post it to you. Is that all right?

Gary Yeah. Of course.

Robert What is it?

Anne You'll find out.

*She turns to **Gary**, holds his hand.*

I like the way you're, you seem, you seem quite sad to me. I quite like that. You should be going.

Gary   Yes.

Anne   Gary, if you find him, when, when you find him. I don't ever want to see him. Because I know I could, I, I could actually *kill* him.

Pause.

The idea that he breathes.

Gary   Yeah.

Anne *addresses the audience.*

Anne   I'm. I'm trying to . . . remember. I'm trying to remember how to walk. Trying to understand how to walk. I'm heading south from the university through Gordon Square and I'm thinking very, very hard about how you put one foot in front of, in front of the other and do you ever, when you, lift both feet?

I am avoiding eye contact.

I have it in my head that the safest thing would be to avoid standing on, on any cracks or gaps in the pavement.

They've started to put up Christmas lights in the trees.

I can smell fire but nobody else seems to notice or be worried so it might just be me.

There's a dry rain on my hair, it's so light that I don't actually even notice it getting wet.

Just on the south-east corner of the square there's a man in a completely white suit. He's very drunk. He's maybe fifty years old. And he's yelling at the sky. He's really furious, really ferocious.

One woman, working in one of the cafés there, she has this smile this big, big, big, big smile. It's lovely.

And all these people are all still cleaning windows. And driving buses. And working in their, in their, their shops. They're all still doing all of that.

I panic about stopping. I decide that I mustn't stop. I mustn't stop. Because I don't know what would happen to me if I stopped. How I would be able to start again.

And I'm getting to the tube station at Russell Square. Right there. Just right in front of it by the fruit stand and the flower stand and the newspaper vendor. By the cinema. With all the people. And the sun comes out.

Gary *and* **Robert** *in a parked car outside a house in Hackney. Lunchtime. The two are completely transfixed by the house they are staking.*

Robert You think it was him?

Pause.

You think he'll come back?

Gary I don't know.

Silence.

Robert Can I tell you something?

Gary Go on.

Robert I was going to put in for a request to transfer. Back up north. Or to another force. I didn't think I could – I got as far as arranging a meeting with the CI. Part of the reason was because you were doing my fucking head in so much.

Gary I see.

Robert I didn't.

Gary No.

Robert I decided not to.

Gary   Good.

Robert   You think we'll get him?

Gary   I don't have a clue.

Some time.

Robert   I finished with Esther.

Gary   You what?

Robert   Last night. Finished it.

Gary   How come?

Robert   It was just. It was getting just too. All the gabbing on about a baby and that. We were just at each other's throats. Yer with me? It was mental.

Gary   Right.

Robert   She cried. Quite badly actually. Did my head in a bit.

Gary   But you didn't let her back.

Robert   No. No. No. I didn't. But fucking drives yer mental, doesn't it?

Gary   Yes. It does.

Robert   Can I ask you something?

Gary   What?

Robert   How long have you known Jenny?

Gary   Since school.

Robert   Long time.

Gary   Not always going out with her all that time.

Robert   No?

Gary   No.

Robert   What is it?

Gary What?

Robert That makes you just know?

Gary What do you mean?

Robert What did you like about her?

Gary Lots of things.

Robert What like?

Gary I always admired the way she did everything properly.

Robert You what?

Gary And then, when she got to about seventeen, almost overnight almost I just thought, 'My God! You are just gorgeous.'

Robert And you still do?

Gary I think so.

Robert Do you love her?

Gary Course.

Robert What do you love about her?

Gary She's very honest. She doesn't put up with any nonsense. Doesn't let me go on. I trust her. (*Beat.*) Sometimes I could just leave her.

Robert Really?

Gary Sometimes I think I've let her down quite badly.

Robert How?

Gary Just . . .

Robert What?

Gary You know what I want to do?

Robert What?

Gary   I want to find the cunts who saw Daisy go and did nothing and just, just, just –

Robert   What?

Gary   Tell them. Ask them what they did. Sometimes I think . . .

Robert   What, Gary?

Gary   I'm not as good at this job as I once was, Robert, you with me?

Long pause.

Robert   You know what I think?

Gary   What?

Robert   What I really think about you?

Gary   What?

Robert   I like the way you can be very honest sometimes. And I think that you are a good copper. Still. But you're a moody fucker. You need to just relax a bit. Tell a few jokes. Stop drinking so much fucking booze and coffee. Cause you'll just die. And stop treating me like I'm a prick. Cause I'm not. Or thinking you can stop all bad things or know people better than they know themselves because you fucking just can't. And I think that you're never going to get away. Go to the Isle of Man. Any of that. It isn't going to happen. That's a bit –

Gary   What?

Robert   I don't know.

Gary   You're quite angry sometimes, aren't you? I quite like that.

Gary *punches* **Robert**'s *arm affectionately but not gently. Turns away.*

Robert   I like you.

Gary You what?

Robert I was going to thank you for not grassing on me when I freaked out on you.

Gary You didn't. Not really.

Robert You're all right. You know? You are. You . . .

Gary What?

Robert Just –

Very, very long pause.

GORSEINON COLLEGE LIBRARY

40400

Lightning Source UK Ltd.
Milton Keynes UK
10 October 2009

144778UK00001B/24/A

9 780413 773654